RE Ideas: Literacy

This book has been devised to provide the RE subject leader with ideas and planning for good quality RE that will also support the whole school aim of improving literacy across the curriculum. In RE we use specialist vocabulary, interpret symbolic language such as simile and metaphor, read and interpret specific styles of text, support pupils in developing and expressing an argument persuasively and effectively – the list could go on. All of this provides an opportunity for pupils to practise regularly, during their learning in RE, the skills and knowledge gained in English and Literacy.

Share this book with your English or Literacy co-ordinator to ensure opportunities for Literacy and RE links can be forged across the subjects. However, in RE we must always ensure that there are clear RE objectives in a lesson. RE lessons should never be simply an opportunity to practise literacy skills.

The book begins with an article that will support the RE subject leader in running staff training on RE and Literacy and provides specific curriculum examples showing how literacy knowledge and skills can be used regularly with 5–11s. For our youngest children we explore how religion shows itself in the home, culminating in opportunities for redesigning the classroom home corner. Mother Teresa is a much studied figure but this unit shares a poetic stimuli and provides opportunities to practise drama and inference skills. The book provides a double-page magazine-style article as a literacy focus for a study of bar and bat mitzvah: we are grateful to the pupils of King Solomon's Academy for this. The work for our older pupils supports the renewed focus in England on debate and discussion in the English curriculum; sharing strategies for improving these skills through RE. Finally there is a selection of links to the use of Literacy strategies in some of our recent curriculum books.

Fiona Moss
Editor

Support material on the RE Today website

The RE Today website offers NATRE members and RE Today subscribers some free additional resources and classroom-ready materials related to this publication. Look out for the 'RE Today on the web' logo at the start of selected articles.

The password for access can be found in each term's *REtoday* magazine or you can use your member/subscriber number.

www.retoday.org.uk

Contents

Our writers and editors are alert to the differences between levels in the four nations of the UK. Our levelled outcomes can be adapted by teachers in their situations, taking account of the Core Syllabus, Religious Education (Northern Ireland) and the National Exemplar Framework for Religious Education, Wales. Specific reference has been made to the outcomes from the Scottish Curriculum for Excellence.

Literacy and RE: why, what and how?

Why link RE to Literacy?

RE should be linked to Literacy when it is appropriate and when both RE outcomes and Literacy outcomes can be fulfilled. Religions and beliefs have a rich literary heritage so linking to Literacy provides opportunities to study the heritage of the particular religion you are teaching about.

Reading, writing, speaking and listening – the four strands of Literacy – can be supported and developed through good RE. However it is essential that RE outcomes and objectives remain the first thing for teachers to consider when planning RE. The links between Literacy and RE are much wider than the specific objectives in the English National Curriculum or programme of study in England, Wales or Northern Ireland or statements in Curriculum for Excellence in Scotland: they link to reading and writing of different genres, discussion, debate, expression of opinion and much more.

As we educate our pupils to be literate we want them to be able to communicate, interpret and respond. This assists pupils in thinking logically and using their imagination and creativity. These skills are fundamental to self-expression and to the understanding of other people.

5 top tips for linking RE and Literacy

- Only make links where both RE and Literacy objectives will be taught well.

- See links as an opportunity to 'steal' extra time for RE. Using RE as the context for some English or Literacy work does not mean you should lose time for RE.

- Ensure RE work is marked first in relation to the RE learning outcomes and then, if appropriate, to Literacy or English outcomes.

- Expect the same standards of literacy in RE as you would in your English or Literacy lessons.

- Don't limit study to sacred texts. Many religious believers today use literacy as a form of expression. Seek out song lyrics, poetry and prose from modern followers of a religion to use as a stimulus.

RE and literacy: short games for encouraging writing in RE

These games are ideal for the beginning or the end of an RE lesson as they consider prior learning or consolidate learning gained in a lesson or unit.

'Call my Bluff'

Choose a series of specialist terms you have used in a lesson or unit of work.

Organise the pupils into groups of three. The group has to come up with three definitions or descriptions of the word. One of the definitions is correct and the other two are not but might have hints of plausibility.

These are read to the class and pupils explain why one of them must be correct and the other two of them cannot be correct, thus showing what they have learnt in the unit.

Reassembling

Choose a short piece of text that the pupils have been studying: a poem, interview, story or extract from sacred text.

This activity can be done with almost all ages by differentiating the text used. At the simplest level it can be done with a four-sentence story.

Cut up the chosen text and photocopy it onto a piece of paper.

Pupils work in pairs to reassemble the text using Literacy and RE knowledge.

Post-its®

During the study of religion and worldviews there is a lot of focus on messages. Whether these are messages that believers find in sacred text or prayer, the message is important for those who practise a religion.

Post-its® allows pupils to consider the message that a person involved in a narrative from sacred text might stick to the fridge or wall, a message that they would like people to remember. For example, what message would Moses have written after receiving the ten commandments, or the doubting men after talking to Guru Gobind Singh in the Sikh story of Bhai Ghanaiya.

RE Today
Services

What to learn and how to learn in RE and Literacy: 4–7s

Linking RE with Literacy and/or the new English curriculum for England provides an op[...]
English skills and can create extra time to teach RE. The following are some examples f[...] ... 4–7 curriculum.

Literacy/English	What could you do in RE?
Listen to and discuss a wide range of poems, stories and non-fiction at a level beyond which they can read independently	Use a story from a faith tradition as a narrative text, e.g. a story of Krishna, the boy Samuel in the temple, Guru Nanak's generosity. Discuss the themes in the narrative. Why are these stories important to believers? Enable pupils to think through the stories by retelling them to each other and in different forms, such as drama, cartoon, dialogue, written, illustrated, hotseating. Use a small number of 'Where is God?' poems from the 2011 Spirited Poetry competition – http://tinyurl.com/k3euxhz – that explore the question of the title. Pupils could use drama, movement and music to represent the ideas in the poems. The children in the class could create their own 'Where is God?' poems.
Become very familiar with key stories…, retelling them and considering their particular characteristics	Use familiar stories such as the story of the birth of Jesus, or the story of Rama and Sita, or the story of Jonah and the Big Fish. Retell them, perhaps from the perspective of different characters. What are the meanings of these stories to people from that particular religion? Alternatively read parables and consider the characteristics of teaching a moral lesson.
Being encouraged to link what they read or hear to their own experiences	In RE we look at social phenomena such as baby naming rituals, weddings and significant places such as places of worship and pilgrimage. After looking at or listening to information about RE content, pupils could make links with their own family experiences of social phenomena and places significant to them. Create charts, photos, diagrams and quotations to put together, as a group, an explanation and glossary.
Making inferences on the basis of what is being said and done and predicting what might happen based on what has been read so far	Many stories that we tell do not give every single detail of what happens – otherwise stories would be too long. Give pupils a couple of scenes from a story from religion and belief and ask them to draw, act out or write what happens between the scenes, e.g. The Milk and the Jasmine Flower – a Sikh story. Further examples of this can be found in the RE Today publication *Share a Story with …*
Compose sentences orally and sequence sentences to form short narratives	Use a jigsaw puzzle depicting a story you are studying from religion and belief. Ask pupils to make the jigsaw and create sentences to describe and tell the story.
Write narratives about personal experiences and those of others (real and fictional)	Narratives from sacred stories often explore a person changing: talk about children going through changes too. These can then provide a stimulus for children writing about their own personal experiences. Use a story such as the story of the Prophet Muhammad (pbuh) and the Old Woman http://www.islamawareness.net/Children/story20.html. Explore the way a character changes as a result of the kindness of others. The story of Zacchaeus would make a good counterpoint to this.
Write about real events, write poetry and write for different purposes	Ask pupils to create a set of six instructions for a minister (or leader in another tradition): 'How to baptise a baby'. You could use the video sequence of baptism from www.request.org.uk or www.bbc.co.uk/education. This can be enacted from the children's instructions, using a doll. Other 'baby welcoming ceremonies' could be used for different groups. It's fun to do 'how not to …' as well, showing the disastrous consequences of not following instructions. Dolls feel no pain! Teach about one or two religious festivals, perhaps Diwali and Eid-ul-Fitr, or Pesach and Easter. As an outcome, get pupils to make a senses poem about what they think it is like for a believer to see, hear, touch, taste, smell, feel and think their way through the festival. Share poems and build a list of sensory experience words.
Provide opportunities for pupils to develop and order their ideas through playing roles and improvising scenes in various settings.	Ask pupils to freeze-frame the most significant moments in a story from religion and belief. Next ask each of the characters what they are thinking about during that moment in the story. Alternatively project the story forward, e.g. how would Zaccheus behave a month after meeting Jesus? Pupils could also act out how a person with particular religious beliefs might act in a particular situation if they were following the teachings of their religion.

What to learn and how to learn in RE and Literacy: 7–11s

Linking RE with Literacy and/or the new English curriculum for England provides an opportunity to practise literacy and English skills and can create extra time to teach RE. The following are some examples from the 7–11 curriculum.

Literacy/English	What could you do in RE?
Listening to and discussing a wide range of fiction, poetry, plays, non-fiction and reference books	Make a habit of using different types of text and book in RE. Set learning tasks that expect pupils to write in different ways, creating plays, biography and references to texts to show and apply their subject knowledge. Pupils could write a short play about an aspect of the life of Abraham, Jesus or the Buddha.
	Pupils consider how some texts from the Torah (e.g. the Shema), the Bible (e.g. 1 Corinthians 13) and the Qur'an (e.g. the First Surah, the Opening) are seen as sources of wisdom in different traditions. They respond to the ideas found in the texts with ideas of their own.
	Pupils compare the texts in the Christian gospels that tell the stories of shepherds and wise men at Jesus' birth, exploring how they are remembered and celebrated in a range of Christmas festivities.
Identifying themes and conventions in a wide range of books	The Bible is a book made up of lots of different types of writing, e.g. letters, parables, rules and laws, and poetry. Collect some extracts from modern translations of the Bible and share examples of some of the different types of writing. Once the type of writing has been identified, ask pupils to think why this book has all these different types of writing in. What is the 'big story' of the Bible?
Recognising some different forms of poetry	Identifying the types of poetry found in sacred text, e.g. psalms in the Old Testament. The example of Psalm 119 could be used. This is often called an acrostic psalm as it was written with eight verses: one for each of the Hebrew consonants in order.
	Pupils find out about different forms of poetry, prayer and meditation in different religions and worldviews, and write some poetry, prayers or meditations suited to particular occasions and traditions.
Drawing inferences such as inferring characters' feelings, thoughts and motives from their actions, and justifying inferences with evidence	Pupils consider how some texts from the Torah (e.g. the Shema), the Bible (e.g. 1 Corinthians 13) and the Qur'an (e.g. The First Surah, the Opening) are seen as sources of wisdom in different traditions. They respond to the ideas found in the texts with ideas of their own.
	Use evidence from the actions of particular religious leaders (including modern-day religious leaders) to identify how members of faiths might try to act in certain situations. Pupils' ideas about this can be shown in the form of role plays, interviews, diary entries and letters from a follower of a faith.
Use drama approaches to understand meaning	Choose a significant part of the story at which to stop the action. Children to represent the characters in tableau at either a moment you choose or the moment they think is significant in a story. The thoughts of each character at this point of the story can then be examined, e.g. Pontius Pilate when he condemns Jesus to death. Examine the thoughts of Jesus, Pontius Pilate, the crowd and the disciples.
Increase familiarity with a wide range of texts … and books from other cultures and traditions	Teaching in RE naturally provides opportunities to use sacred text but also texts and books that show, for example, Christianity as a worldwide faith. Remember – when using a story that is important to a particular religion or belief community – to ensure you consider what meaning from the story you want the pupils to learn about. Not all stories are about being nice to people!

RE Today Services

Literacy/English	What could you do in RE?
Discuss and evaluate how authors use language, including figurative language, considering the impact on the reader	Study parables from the Bible as an example of analogies, e.g. the story of the Lost Son where the father represents God and the lost son represents people who are no longer following God. Give pupils another parable and see if they can interpret the analogies used.
	Study some of the metaphors used to describe Jesus in the gospel of John known as the 'I am' sayings: e.g. the light of the world, the bread of life, the gate, the good shepherd, the true vine, the way, the truth and the life.
Use technical terms such as metaphor, simile, analogy, imagery, etc.	Use the Jewish PARDES approach to interpret a text such as one of the ten commandments. First interpret at a literal level, P'shat. Next interpret at a deeper level, Remez. In pairs ask pupils to discuss the deeper ideas and make a drama, D'rash, to express one scenario. Finally explore the hidden, Sod – this might be the consequences.
Distinguish between statements of fact and opinion	The thinking skills strategy of fact or opinion is used when the material used is controversial, for example the idea of a religious belief. It encourages children to think about what is a fact, a belief or an opinion. For example, collect about 20 pieces of text about prayer in Islam. Put each piece of information onto a separate card. Include some information about prayer, e.g. Muslims try to pray at least five times a day; some comments from people, e.g. 'When I pray I am worshipping God and I am talking to Allah' or 'Prayer is very powerful' and some quotes from sacred text.
	Ask pupils to work in groups to discuss each card and sort the cards into two piles 'fact or opinion' or even three piles 'fact, opinion or belief'. They need to be able to justify their choices. Would a Muslim or a Christian make the same choice? Why/Why not?
Explain and discuss what they have read, including through formal presentations and debates	Pupils research the Hindu concept of ahimsa (non-violence), and explain and describe the impact of Hindu teaching about harmlessness on questions about what people eat and how people treat animals. They explain what they have researched and express their own ideas in debates and presentations.
	Pupils discuss and debate reasons why different people have different ideas about the divine, e.g. whether God is real and what God is like.
Provide reasoned justification for their views	Pupils compare how different religions and beliefs, e.g. Christians, Muslims, Hindus or Humanists celebrate a marriage. In discussion or writing pupils express and argue for ideas of their own about the purposes of marriage.
	Pupils apply their own ideas about justice and fairness to the work of three development charities such as Christian Aid, Islamic Relief and Oxfam, presenting this work in a suitable written or oral format.
Skills of information retrieval, e.g. information leaflets	Use a selection of information books and a visit to a local place of worship, e.g. mosque or church or both, to create a leaflet about the purposes of a place of worship. This task requires retrieval and research skills as well as information processing and writing skills.
Identifying audience and purpose for writing, selecting the appropriate form and using similar writing as models for their own	Pupils write persuasively or as a balanced debate about the reasons why people who have a particular religious background or non-religious worldview try to help people who are vulnerable (e.g. victims of natural disasters or prejudice, people who live with disabilities or people affected by war).
	Use modern short forms of expressing opinions and ideas such as tweets. If Sita was a tweeter what would Sita tweet?

Homes: what do they tell us about how people pray?

Background knowledge for teachers

The home is the starting point for this unit, with all pupils reflecting upon where they live. This extends to allow pupils to look into the homes of children from three specific faith backgrounds (Christianity, Hinduism and Islam) and consider what they might find in each. Teachers are encouraged to help pupils make links between each of the three homes studied and their own lives – some of the furniture, possessions and activities in the pictures are quite generic for this purpose.

There is a focus on what can be seen relating to prayer in each of the three homes, looking especially at a puja tray in Hinduism, prayer beads in Islam and grace before meals in Christianity. Although the pictures show artefacts linked to prayer, it is beneficial for the class teacher to have real versions of these artefacts in the classroom as well.

After an activity based on similarities between prayer in the three homes, pupils are encouraged to think of words of prayer that might go into a special book for the home corner. The home corner is used to reinforce learning throughout the whole of this unit, pulling together what children have found out about all three homes alongside experiences of their own households.

Most of the four main purposes for Christian prayer (praise, give thanks, say sorry and ask) are covered in this unit and all four can be incorporated into the final activity depending on pupils' ability.

Essential knowledge for pupils

Pupils should know that:

- their own homes are similar to and different from those of others
- some people pray in their homes and may use special objects to help them when praying
- there are different ways of praying
- prayer is a way in which people try to communicate with God.

Links to Literacy and English

Pupils will have opportunities to:

- participate in discussions, listening and responding appropriately to adults and their peers
- ask relevant questions to extend their understanding and knowledge
- write sentences and discuss what they have written with the teacher or other pupils
- read their writing aloud clearly enough to be heard by their peers and the teacher.

Assessment for Learning

This section shows some of the outcomes achievable by pupils of different abilities in the 4–6 age range.

Level	Description of achievement: I can ...
ELGs Almost all pupils in this age group	- talk about important things in the home(s) that my family lives in - notice ways in which Samit, Imran and Grace's homes are similar to and different from my own - talk simply about prayer - write some simple words that could be used in prayer.
1 The most able pupils in this age group	- name some items used in prayer in Hinduism and Islam and talk about how they are used - recognise that prayer is a way in which people talk to God and use my understanding to compose some good words for prayer - *talk about objects and activities in my own home and in Samit, Imran and Grace's homes.*

This unit helps pupils in Scotland to achieve RME 0-06a and RME 1-06a.

Web support

An explanation of each of the items found on a puja tray:

See: www.crickweb.co.uk/ks2re.html

Information about prayer beads in Islam;

See: www.strath.ac.uk/redb/notes/islam/tasbi/

Subscribers and NATRE members can also download the following from the RE Today website: www.retoday.org.uk

- pictures of children and their houses from p.9
- photographs of how to set up a home corner.

RE Today Services

What is special in our homes?

Ask pupils to bring in a photograph of a room in their home. Share these photos as a class and use them to initiate discussion focusing on what pupils like about their home and special items found within it (both religious and not).

Lead a discussion with the pupils:

- What is your favourite thing in the picture?
- Is that a picture of your favourite place in your home?
- What objects do you have in your home that are very special indeed?
- Is there anything that you must be very careful with or are not allowed to touch – why do you think that is?
- In your home, is there anything that makes you think about God?
- Is there anything at home that helps you think about praying?

Give pupils a picture of a house with 2–4 windows in it. The number of windows depends on the ability of the pupil. In each window, ask pupils to draw one special object they have in their home that a passer-by might see if they peeped in through the window.

Support pupils to label or write a sentence describing each one. The houses could be displayed in a row to resemble a street.

Samit's home – praying in a Hindu home

Introduce Samit, who is from a Hindu family. Explain that children are going to find out about his home. Display the picture of a room from Samit's home but ensure that it is covered up so children cannot see it yet. Use a 'through the keyhole' strategy to reveal parts of the picture one by one and ask pupils to say what they can see.

Discuss with pupils how there are objects within the picture that we find in most homes, while some others might be less familiar to many pupils. Focus on any objects that pupils cannot readily identify – what do they think these might be?

Examining artefacts

Concentrate on the shrine and puja tray, allowing pupils to see a real puja tray too. Ask pupils to state what they can say about it and what they think it is for.

Sit in a circle around the puja tray. Show the objects on the tray and help pupils understand how Samit and his family might use each of them when they pray.

Play 'What's missing?' game. Teacher shows puja tray with one object missing. Children show visually which object is absent by drawing it or writing the word, depending on their ability. Pupils should then orally explain how the object is used in prayer.

Discuss the five senses and encourage pupils to use all five while learning about the puja tray. Ask pupils to identify what Samit would be able to see, hear, touch, taste and smell during puja.

Activity 3 — Imran's home – thinking about God

Show the pupils the picture of a room in Imran's house on p.9. Discuss with pupils what objects they can easily name and which they do not know so much about.

Gathering information

Help pupils to create questions regarding what they would like to know about objects in the picture of Imran's house. If pupils do not naturally ask questions about the Qur'an, Qur'an stand, prayer mat and prayer beads, gently direct them to do so.

Ensure pupils' questions are answered in a way that will engage your class. For example, use a Muslim persona doll to answer the questions or give the answers in the form of a letter written to the class by Imran.

Thinking about prayer beads

Point out the prayer beads, known as tasbih or subha beads, that help Muslims such as Imran to focus on the 99 names of Allah. It would be useful to have a set of prayer beads for pupils to see and touch in the classroom. Explain that for each bead, one of Allah's 99 names is said and that each name shows one thing about God.

Introduce some of the 99 names, for example The First, The All Powerful, The Knower of All, The Generous and The Loving One, and discuss with children what each might really mean. Give pupils some time to reflect upon what the names of Allah might show about God and what they might already know and think about God for themselves.

Applying learning

Arrange for pupils make their own string of 5–10 beads perhaps using wooden beads or pasta. For each bead, they should state one thing they think a Muslim could say about God. These strings of beads can be placed into the class home corner.

Discuss how both Samit and Imran had objects in their homes that helped them to think about God and pray, but that these objects were not the same.

Activity 4 — Grace's home – a prayer of thanks

With pupils, focus on the picture of Grace and her family at home. Draw children's attention to the books including the Bible, explaining that it is a holy book for Grace and her family – do the pupils remember another child who had a holy book in his house?

Look closely at the image and through questioning focus on when pupils' own families enjoy spending time together, either at mealtimes like Grace's family or other times, how Grace's family are eating a meal together and what pupils think they are doing before eating.

Explain that Grace's family are Christians and, like many Christian families, they are saying a prayer of thanks before eating their meal. Listen to some examples of prayers traditionally said at grace before meals, see p.11, and see if pupils can pick out messages of thanks in the prayers. If pupils have not already done so, point out that Grace's name is the same as the prayer – why do pupils think this might be?

Use images from the internet of placemats with examples of graces on. Look at some with pupils, examples might be from www.gracesettings.com/collections/grace-mats or www.christianaid.org.uk/Images/Harvest-placemat-June-2014.pdf.

Ask pupils to think of five things that Grace might want to say thank you for and draw them to create a pictorial prayer for Grace to use at mealtimes. More able pupils can mix images of thanks and praise. The pictorial prayers can be turned into placemats that Grace might like to use by mounting on card or laminating.

RE Today Services

Samit's home. Shrines in Hindu homes are located in clean rooms and are therefore often found in bedrooms or kitchens. Samit's is in the spare bedroom. The puja tray and shrine can be seen in this picture.

A closer look at the puja tray in Samit's home

Sitting room in Imran's house with prayer mat, Qur'an, Qur'an stand and tasbih

A close-up of Imran's Qur'an, Qur'an stand and tasbih

Grace's family at home, saying grace before eating their meal

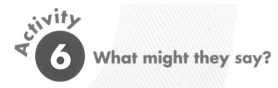

Activity 5 — In the box

Put two linked artefacts that pupils have seen from pictures of houses into a mystery box. These could be objects from the same household, such as a bell and pot of water which are both used in Hindu prayer, or different ones such as a prayer card (Christian) and prayer beads (Muslim) which are used in prayer. In pairs, pupils discuss what they think the link might be between the two artefacts and then report back.

Have a range of artefacts that pupils have encountered throughout this unit ready. These could include a puja set, prayer beads, prayer mat, Qur'an stand, Bible and cross. Children work in pairs and small groups to select a pair of linked artefacts to go into the mystery box and give the reasons for their choice. Please note it would not be appropriate to put a copy of the Qur'an into the box.

Activity 6 — What might they say?

Acting

Act out with children ways in which people talk to each other: examples could include, sitting and chatting, talking on the telephone, shouting across the playground or sending an email.

Discussing

Ask children to remind you what they know about how Imran, Samit and Grace pray. Ensure pupils are familiar with the idea that although people might pray in different ways, prayer itself is a way in which people talk to God.

Visualising

Ask children to close their eyes and remember the three family homes that they have looked at recently.

Ask them to try to imagine Samit and his family doing puja at their shrine. Next think of Imran and his family praying using prayer mats and also concentrating on Allah using the prayer beads. Finally remember Grace and her family saying a prayer together before eating.

Ask pupils to keep their eyes closed while they remember that sometimes people think of how wonderful God is when praying, just as they learnt with Imran's family and the prayer beads. At other times people say thank you to God when praying, just as they learnt with Grace's family.

If appropriate, introduce the idea that sometimes people say sorry when praying, too. Before opening their eyes, ask pupils to think about a message for God that a religious person might like to say. The message might thank God, praise him or say sorry for something.

Purposeful writing

After pupils have finished thinking of messages independently, discuss some of the class's ideas together and if appropriate write some down together as shared writing. Pupils can then write their own message that a person might like to say while praying. Encourage pupils to write it beautifully as it will go into the class's very own special book.

Once finished, pupils can read out the message that they wrote. After the messages have been stuck into the class's special book, it can be kept in the home corner as a reminder of the holy books in the homes that pupils have learnt about. Taking inspiration from the Muslim home, pupils might want to choose a place in the home corner for this book that shows its important status.

RE Today Services

Grace

Examples of prayers said at grace can be found in many books and on many websites. Two examples are:

Father in heaven, who is great and good,

Thank you for my family and my food.

Guide and help me in all the things I do,

Bless this day and all those who love me too.

Thank you for the food we are about to eat. We give thanks that we are not hungry or thirsty, let us remember how lucky we are.

Continuous provision

This unit offers many opportunities for continuous provision activities.

- **Being the boss!** Using artefacts from the puja tray, or pictures of them, children take turns in being the boss and instructing others on how Samit would use each item. Pupils can act out being Samit, following the instruction given by the boss – work out together whether the boss gave a good instruction or not.

- **Thinking and threading:** Put out beads and string so that pupils can have another attempt at the activity based on Islamic prayer beads – perhaps this time, they might like to thread a different amount of beads or remember different names that Muslims use for Allah. As long as pupils have attempted the activity about the names of Allah (Activity 2) during class time, in continuous provision this activity might have a different focus with pupils threading 5–10 beads and saying 5–10 good qualities that their friend or a family member possesses.

- **Meaningful messages:** Pupils can carry on adding special words and messages to God to a special book during continuous provision. The home corner in the photos has two identical golden special books. The first was written and completed during Activity 6 and is displayed on the table, while the second is near the writing implements to be filled in as the children wish. This hopefully ensures that, during continuous provision time, nothing untoward happens to the first book containing the children's best work from Activity 6.

Role play area or home corner

These photographs show how a home corner can be built upon throughout the unit. Members and subscribers can access more images showing the steps towards completing this home corner on the RE Today website.

Before Activity 1 – a generic home corner

After Activity 3 – with the addition of items from Imran's home: prayer mat, Qur'an stand, topees and strings of prayer beads made by pupils are also added

Why do some people inspire others?

Background knowledge for teachers

Many religions encourage compassion in their sources of wisdom, scriptures and community life. But most faiths use story to teach compassion, and use inspiring key figures to share the values of the faith. Mother Teresa of Kolkata is not universally admired – there are critics. But she is very widely recognised as a person of great compassion and great influence. This work offers pupils aged 6–9 some Literacy- and English-linked ways of using her story to reflect on profound issues. See the work as a simple introduction to some 'deep stuff'.

This work uses skills that matter in Literacy and the English curriculum to explore religious material: drama, poetry, creative work and thinking skills such as inferring and giving simple reasons for their ideas. These approaches are intended to build up understanding and insight by revisiting some profound key concepts in different ways, through team work, drama, poetry and discussion.

Links to Literacy and English

This work uses skills that matter in Literacy and the English curriculum to explore religious material. Drama, poetry, creative work and thinking skills such as inferring and giving simple reasons for their ideas. The English curriculum for 6–7 year olds in England says:

'Teachers should make sure that pupils:

- listen to and discuss a wide range of stories, poems, plays and information books

- participate in discussion about books, poems and other works, taking turns and listening to what others say

- explain and discuss their understanding of books, poems and other material.'

This work enables all these outcomes to be targeted.

The English curriculum for 7–9 year olds in England says:

'Teachers should make sure that pupils are:

- understanding what they read, by checking that the text makes sense to them, by discussing their understanding and by explaining the meaning of words in context

- asking questions to improve their understanding of a text

- drawing inferences such as inferring characters' feelings, thoughts and motives from their actions, and justifying inferences with evidence

- predicting what might happen from details stated and implied.'

This work enables all these outcomes to be targeted.

Assessment for Learning

This section shows some of the outcomes achievable by pupils of different abilities in the 6–9 age range.

Level	Description of achievement: I can ...
2 Almost all pupils in this age group	• outline the main events of the story of the life of Mother Teresa • suggest the meaning of some of Mother Teresa's ideas and prayers • respond sensitively to things Jesus said and to things Mother Teresa did and said.
3 Many pupils in this age group	• describe ways in which Mother Teresa put Jesus' teaching into action, using Bible quotes to infer ideas • make connections between Mother Teresa's life and the idea of 'inspiration' • find out more about, and describe, my own 'inspiring people'.
4 The most able pupils in this age group	• apply ideas such as 'saint', 'follower', 'compassion,' or 'inspiration' to my understanding of Mother Teresa's life • infer meaning from the story of Mother Teresa, making reasoned connections to sayings of Jesus and to their own ideas • investigate and explore in depth the question: 'Who is inspiring for me, and why?'

This unit helps pupils in Scotland to achieve RME 1-02b and RME 1-09c.

Essential knowledge for pupils

Pupils should know:

- some Christian ideas about inspiration and about how and why Christians want to follow Jesus

- that belief in God can be demonstrated in a range of ways.

 ## Web support

NATRE members and subscribers can also download the following from the RE Today website:

- a PowerPoint sequence to support this unit of work
- a PDF of pages 17, 18 and 19.

Activity 1 Still images

This activity is recommended for Literacy with 6–7 year olds. It needs sensitive handling, but opens up imaginative learning well. Here it is used to explore Mother Teresa's life story, and some related ideas.

Put the class in six small groups of four or five, and set them the task of co-operating to make four still images (tableaux) in their group. Tell them these will be photographed, and everyone will be able to look at them and learn more about the story. The children will be given four parts of the story to think about. It's a great idea to have a plain cloth as a backdrop hanging against a wall behind the scenes. It may be worthwhile asking the children to wear a white tee shirt, or perhaps plain school uniform will be just as good. Tell them the point is all about the body language, and faces, arms, fingers and postures really matter. Each team does all four images. Give them just four or five minutes to get their 'Still Image' ready to be photographed. Read out each of the scenarios at the bottom of the page to them to get them started.

When the teams in the class have all made their Still Image photographs, put them into a slideshow and talk about what each group have done well. Ask a good talker from each team to narrate the incident of the picture they have made. Print off the page, and ask pupils to draw think bubbles for each of the characters in their Still Image. They add some single words to the bubbles to show what each person would be thinking.

To add a deeper dimension to the Still Image work, put the children back into teams and ask them to make an image of an idea, rather than a scene. These ideas might work well: peace/care/harmony/listening/compassion/ inspiration. Encourage them to try out all the ideas they can think of before developing one for another photograph.

A third round could ask pupils to make a Still Image from one of Mother Teresa's famous sayings – see several examples on pp.16 and 17.

A When Mother Teresa was 18 she decided to become a nun. She knelt at the altar in a church, and her family supported her as she gave her life to God.

B One day, when Mother Teresa was a headmistress, aged 36, she saw a man dying in the gutter, in the street. Others just ignored him, but she knelt down and took his hand. She prayed for him.

C In 1950 Mother Teresa set up a new community of nuns. She was the leader. At first, there were five of them, and she guided their lives to follow Jesus. They were called 'The Missionaries of Charity' and promised to help everyone in need.

D In 1979 Mother Teresa was given the Nobel Peace Prize. She flew to Norway and spoke to a huge crowd in Oslo. She gave everyone in the crowd a prayer card which said 'Lord, make me a channel of your peace, that where there is hatred I may bring love.'

Mother Teresa's Nobel Speech can be seen in full at www.nobelprize.org/mediaplayer/index.php?id=1852 It lasts under 20 minutes, and any class would benefit from seeing a small section. The first four minutes work well.

Activity 2 — Six things Jesus said: inferring ideas

Tell the class that they are going to learn about Mother Teresa, an inspiring Christian who tried to follow Jesus. Show them a picture. To begin with they have to try and work out how she might have tried to follow Jesus.

Using p.15, remind them of six sentences Jesus said, and talk about what they mean: it's a good idea to have these sentences on large flash cards or on the whiteboard. How would a person behave if they were trying to follow Jesus?

Next read out the five examples of events from Mother Teresa's life, and ask the children, in paired discussion, to guess what she might do. After talking through these five, ask the class: was she a good follower of Jesus? What did they like best that she did? This activity probably works best for 6–7 year olds.

Activity 4 — Inspiring words

Introduce pupils to the poem Mother Teresa adapted called 'Anyway'. She had a version similar to this on her wall. This is a slightly simplified version. Use copies of p.17 for this.

There are eight tasks to support learning about the poem, ways of using and developing literacy skills in handling a text of this type. Pupils should tackle at least four of these tasks: giving them some choice is a good plan, as it motivates all pupils a little more.

Activity 6 — Applying the concept of 'sainthood' – extending the learning for higher-achieving pupils

Pupils are often a bit hazy about different Christian groups such as Catholics or Methodists. Teach them that the Pope, the leader of all the world's Catholic Christians, can recognise a person who has died as a saint.

The activity shown on p.19 gives small groups of higher-achieving pupils an extra task, a way of thinking about this that applies criteria to the story they have studied. As of 2015, there is one miracle attributed to praying to Mother Teresa. The Catholic Church is waiting for another to be recognised.

Activity 3 — A class art book of Mother Teresa's life

Tell the class Mother Teresa's life story – make the storytelling exciting, and focus on the parts about God. You can use p.16 for the outline, but more detail is easily available online.

Blow up the text of p.16, and cut it into 24 cards. You could do some sequencing activities if you wanted to. Children should be given time and space to each make one page picture of one of the sentences, then arrange them into a class book or gallery of her life.

The activity can be easily differentiated: the cards with sayings from Mother Teresa are harder to visualise. Give them to children who are ready for a challenge.

Activity 5 — Ranking reasons for inspiration

When pupils have done all these tasks, have another class discussion about the idea of 'inspiration'. Tell the children it is a word about 'breathing in'. Some inspiring people are breathtaking! We can be inspired by sports stars, music heroes or people who are brilliant at what they do, but many people say Mother Teresa is inspiring for her faith, hope and love.

- What do the children think?

Talk through the eight ideas cards on p.18 with the class, and then ask them to work in threes:

- agree their own 'Top Five' in their own 'right order'
- stick them to a card, and write next to them the reasons why they put these five top.

This is a good piece of evidence for assessment if you need it.

RE Today Services

Activity 2 — Six things Jesus said: inferring ideas

Mother Teresa really wanted to follow Jesus. Here are six famous things that Jesus said. Discuss them together, then see if the pupils can infer what Mother Teresa did to try and follow Jesus in different situations. You might put them on large flash cards in the centre of a circle of pupils.

Jesus said:

Trust in God.	Love your neighbour as much as you love yourself.	If someone does you harm, forgive them.
Do to other people what you would like them to do to you.	Happy are those who are kind to others. People will be kind to them.	**Be like a light: shine in a dark world.**

So can you guess what Mother Teresa did when …?

Ask the pupils to listen to each of the scenarios below – you might read them aloud twice, and have a thinking pause in between. Ask children to talk with a partner about what Teresa might have done if she wanted to follow Jesus. Lower-achieving pupils could be given alternatives. The right-hand column says what she did.

After all the pupils have guessed or inferred the answers, see if they can link up what Mother Teresa did to the sayings of Jesus.

One day in 1946 when she was a headmistress Teresa was walking down the street in Kolkata. She saw a person lying in the gutter. He was dirty, starving and terribly ill. He was close to death. Everyone else was ignoring the man.	She took the man's hand, spoke kindly to him, and prayed for him. She stayed with him till he died, and arranged for his body to be cremated.
Mother Teresa was always very busy. Thousands of people came to her homes for help when they were sick or dying. There was never enough money to look after all those she wanted to help. She did not want to beg.	She got up at 5 a.m. every morning and prayed to God to supply the needs of the Missionaries of Charity.
Some people did not like the fact that Mother Teresa was caring for sick and dying people in their area. They worried they might catch something nasty. Some of them threw stones at her.	She forgave the people throwing stones. She asked them to come and see the work she was doing. She took them on a tour of her 'Home for people dying'. One of them became her friend.
Mother Teresa knew that some people in India had babies they did not want. Sometimes these babies were just left outside a hospital by mums who were too poor to look after them.	She put adverts in the papers to say 'If you cannot care for your baby, if you don't want your baby, I want her, or him. Bring the babies to me.' She ran the biggest adoption agency in India.
One day Mother Teresa met a person who had the virus called HIV. Many people were scared of this virus, which can make you very ill or kill you. They would not even shake hands with a person with HIV.	She sat down with the sick person and held his hand while they were filmed and the film was shown on TV. She was not scared.

A life story in 24 pieces

Pupils can take one piece each and make a work of art, then create a class book of the 24 pages they made. Call it 'An Inspiring Life in Pictures.' Obviously some of these are easier than others to draw and illustrate. Teachers can differentiate who gets which card, and give the harder sayings, for example, to the higher-achieving pupils.

Tiny baby Agnes was born in 1910 in Macedonia.	Teresa held the dying man's hand. He said 'It is a very long time since anyone touched me.'	All over Kolkata, thousands of the saddest and poorest people were loved by Mother Teresa.
When she was a little girl, she liked stories about people who gave their lives to God.	Teresa took people who were dying alone in Kolkata and nursed them herself.	Mother Teresa became famous all over the world, teaching love and peace.
When she was 18, Agnes committed herself to serve God as a Sister, a nun.	At first, Teresa worked alone to help the poorest of the poor. She was poor too, and had to beg.	Mother Teresa always got up before dawn to pray for God's help in her work.
Agnes went to India to be a teacher. She lived in the mountains.	In 1950 the Pope agreed that Teresa could set up a new group of nuns: the Missionaries of Charity.	Mother Teresa loved children, and always took in any baby who had no home.
Agnes chose a new name for herself as a nun: Teresa.	Mother Teresa says 'God doesn't require us to succeed. He just requires us to try.'	Mother Teresa died in 1997. One day she might become 'Saint Teresa'.
Sister Teresa was such a good teacher she became a headmistress at a school in Kolkata.	Mother Teresa says 'Do something beautiful for God.'	Today there are over 5500 Missionaries of Charity who work all over the world.
One day in 1946 she felt God telling her to help the poorest people in Kolkata. Her life changed.	Mother Teresa says: 'If you cannot feed one hundred people, then just feed one.'	The Missionaries of Charity care for the poorest people by running hospitals and children's homes.
She saw a man dying from a horrible disease in the gutter of the street.	'Don't be satisfied with giving money to charity. Instead spread your love everywhere you go.'	Mother Teresa said: 'I am a pencil in God's hand. God is writing a love letter to the world.'

RE Today Services

Task 1: Read aloud

Read the poem out loud in your group. Two voices can do this, taking alternate lines.

Task 2: Choose music

Can you think of a tune for these words, or some music to use as backing for a reading?

Task 3: Image slides

Can you choose 8 pictures to go into a PowerPoint slideshow that also has these words in it? Make the PowerPoint.

Task 4: Discuss

Here are some questions to think about and discuss.

- Which bits of Mother Teresa's advice do you agree with most strongly? Why?
- Can you think of anyone you know who seems to follow some of the advice Mother Teresa gives in the poem?
- Do you agree with Mother Teresa that our lives are between us and God, not other people?
- Is this an inspiring poem? If you think it is, try to say why.
- What is the hardest thing Mother Teresa's poem advises?

Anyway

A poem adapted by Mother Teresa

People are often unkind and selfish:
Forgive them anyway.
If you are kind, people may think
you want something back:
Be kind anyway.
If you are honest, people may cheat you:
Be honest anyway.
If you find happiness, people may be jealous:
Be happy anyway.
The good you do today may be forgotten tomorrow:
Do good anyway.
Give the world the best you have, and it may never be enough:
Give your best anyway.
For you see, in the end, it is between you and God.
It was never between you and them, anyway.

Adapted from Kent Keith, *Do it Anyway*, New World Library 2003.

Task 5: Ask a grown-up

Take your copy of the poem and talk to a grown-up at home about it. Ask the person you choose these questions:

- What do you like about this advice?
- What advice here is hard to take?
- Do you agree with Mother Teresa about God, or do you have a different idea?
- If you chose some inspiring words (maybe similar to these) what would you choose?

Task 8: Display

Collect the work other people have done in Tasks 1–7 and plan a classroom or school hall display to show what you all think of Mother Teresa's Prayer. You could call it 'Inspiring Words'!

Task 6: Giving your own good advice

Create some lines of advice of your own to give to people when life is tough. Mother Teresa did eight lines, but can you think of four good ones? (Don't copy hers!)

Task 7: Calligraphy

Make the most beautiful written version of this poem that you can. What designs, lettering styles and art techniques can you use to make it really sensational?

5 Mother Teresa: what makes her inspiring?

Tim Graham / Alamy

Mother Teresa was inspiring because she could hear God's voice, and she did what God said.	Mother Teresa was inspiring because she lived a life of love.
Mother Teresa was inspiring because she cared for the people everyone else ignored.	Mother Teresa was inspiring because she tried to be like Jesus.
Mother Teresa was inspiring because she never gave up.	Mother Teresa was inspiring because she trusted God and she wasn't scared of anything.
Mother Teresa was inspiring because she could have had an easy life but she chose a hard life.	Mother Teresa was inspiring because she prayed every day and God helped her.

Give pairs of pupils these eight ideas to cut up and rank these eight suggestions, then ask them to make fours to disagree and refine their ideas.

To extend the learning, ask them to select another great human leader, and suggest eight reasons why their choice is inspiring to others.

RE Today Services

Mother Teresa: Is she a saint?

What is a saint?

In the Roman Catholic Church, a person may be recognised as a saint after they have died. This Church, led by His Holiness the Pope, say that you can recognise a saint.

These five questions are a way of considering if a person is a saint:

1 Did the person serve God?
2 Is the person a fine example of faith?
3 Is the person a fine example of hope?
4 Is the person a fine example of love?
5 Has anyone prayed to God for a miracle, through this person, since she or he died, and had their prayer answered?

Describe your ideas in the boxes below.

This stained glass window of Mother Teresa comes from her home country of Macedonia, in southern Europe.

© zatletic - fotolia.com

Do you think Mother Teresa served God? (Say why)	Do you think Mother Teresa was a fine example of faith? (Say why)	Do you think Mother Teresa was a fine example of hope? (Say why)
Do you think Mother Teresa was a fine example of love? (Say why)	**Do you think prayers to Mother Teresa might be answered? (Say why)**	**Do you think Mother Teresa should be recognised as a saint? (Say why)**

Why do young Jewish people make promises?

Background knowledge for teachers

Bar and bat mitzvah are extremely significant rites of passage as they mark the move from childhood towards adulthood. After becoming bar/bat mitzvah – son or daughter of the commandment – young people are considered responsible for their own decisions and actions and old enough to follow the mitzvot (commandments) for themselves.

In Orthodox Jewish communities boys become bar mitzvah at the age of 13 and the ceremony is often held on the Sabbath after their birthday. They prepare by learning about the religion in special classes and learning to read their portion of the Torah in Hebrew. Within the service a boy will read his portion at the bimah (raised platform), and often process around the synagogue with the scrolls. He will also often be given a tallit (prayer shawl) and tefillin, a black leather box containing text from the Jewish Bible which is worn on the arm or forehead. At the age of 12 a girl becomes bat mitzvah: she will also prepare for the day through classes and on the day she will make a speech about the portion of Torah being read on the day or another important topic.

In non-Orthodox – sometimes known as Jewish progressive – communities, both boys and girls take part in bar/bat mitzvah at 13 to show equality. They both go to special classes and read their portion of the Torah at the bimah.

This unit provides interviews with Jewish children as a resource to explore the significance and meaning of these ceremonies for Jewish communities.

Essential knowledge for pupils

Pupils should know:

- becoming bar and bat mitzvah is a significant milestone in the life of a Jewish person
- bar/bat mitzvah means son/daughter of the commandment and its significance for Jewish people
- what happens during a bar and bat mitzvah service and the significance of these actions and objects.

Links to the English curriculum and Literacy

The activities in this unit support pupils with

- using simple organisational devices in non narrative material
- asking questions to improve their understanding of the text
- identifying the main ideas drawn from more than one paragraph and summarising them.

Assessment for Learning

This section shows some of the outcomes achievable by pupils of different abilities in the 7–9 age range.

Level	Description of achievement: I can ...
2 Almost all pupils in this age group	• give a reason why bar/bat mitzvah is significant to Jewish people • gather and select from pieces of information about bar/bat mitzvah to share my understanding of this important time • suggest meanings for different actions and objects used during bar/bat mitzvah.
3 Many pupils in this age group	• make links between the Jewish commandments and becoming bar/bat mitzvah • describe what happens at bar and bat mitzvah, linking it to following commandments and becoming an adult • *ask questions and suggest answers that Jewish people might give to the significance of becoming bar/bat mitzvah.*
4 The most able pupils in this age group	• describe how bar/bat mitzvah might feel to the young Jewish person, comparing it with the emotions of another rite of passage. • show that I understand how becoming bar/bat mitzvah might affect the life of a Jewish person.

This unit helps pupils in Scotland to achieve RME 1-06a and 1-06b.

 Web support

The Jewish Way of Life DVD is very useful to show the importance of bar and bat mitzvah:

See: www.reonline.org.uk/specials/jwol/

BBC Bitesize has a short clip on the traditions of bar mitzvah which is suitable for this age group:

See: www.bbc.co.uk/education/clips/zm7tfg8

NATRE members and *REtoday* subscribers can also download the following from the RE Today website:

- a copy of the magazine article on p.22–3
- a copy of the tallit template on p.25
- a copy of the active reading grid on p.25.

RE Today Services

Activity 1 — Identifying milestones

Ask the pupils to work in pairs to create a list of the most important things that have happened to them so far in life. Model some examples before discussions start, e.g. being born, learning to ride a bicycle, passing a test or joining Brownies. Discuss some of the examples that the pupils suggest:

- Why are they important?
- Are some more important than others? Why?

As a class, think of some of the milestones that the pupils will encounter. Choose 10, a selection of those that have happened and those that will happen in the future. Write each one on a card.

Bring in a selection of 10 stones and rocks from tiny to large. As a class, attribute one milestone to each of the rocks. Choose the largest rock for the most important and the smallest rock for the least important. Put them in the order that these things will happen. Discuss with pupils why they think some are more important than others.

Remind the pupils of some of the religions you have learnt about. Ask them to think about some of the milestones that happen in the life of someone from that religion.

Activity 3 — Research and act

Use the resource *Jewish Way of Life*.
See: www.reonline.org.uk/specials/jwol/
Select 'Time' from the menu and then 'Life cycle'.

Show pupils the section about the bar and bat mitzvah of David and Sarah. There is also a film on BBC Bitesize on the traditions of bar mitzvah
See: www.bbc.co.uk/education/clips/zm7tfg8

Arrange the pupils into small groups and ask them to write a series of questions for either David or Sarah to answer about their bar or bat mitzvah. Next, ask the groups to write responses from David and Sarah to the questions they have written.

Ask pupils to turn their interviews into a radio broadcast in the Meaningful Milestones series with the title 'Why Bar/Bat Mitzvah is Important to Me'.

Allow each group to 'perform' their interview to the rest of the class.

Activity 2 — Active reading

For these activities you will need each pair of pupils to have a copy of the 'Meaningful milestones' activity on pp.22–3.

Explain to the pupils that you are going to find out about a milestone in the life of a Jewish person. Ask the pupils to work in pairs.

Summarising

Read the text of p.22 to pupils and ask them to sum up what they have heard in one sentence.

Next give the text of p.22 to each pair.

Ask them to:

- underline any words that they think someone would need to find out more about
- write no more than three sentences that summarise what they have read.

Digging deeper

Give each pair a copy of the two interviews on p.23. Ask each pupil to read one interview and summarise what they have found out using the thinking frame on p.25. After filling in the thinking frame, pupils explain to their partner what they found out from their interview and identify and describe similarities and differences.

Please note that the interview with Sarah is simpler than the interview with Elliot.

Defining

Go back to the words they underlined on p.22. Underline any words that require defining on p.23. Using www.reonline.org.uk/specials/jwol/ and any books or additional resources, create a glossary of terms that could be added to the magazine article.

Meaningful milestones

Elliot and Sarah share with us an important milestone in their lives

Welcome to the latest in our series of articles where we explore an important day in one of our readers' lives and learn about the day through their eyes.

For many young people who belong to a religious group, the day you make promises for yourself about what you believe is extremely significant. For many Christians, promises are made as a teenager during confirmation. In the Sikh community, the Amrit Sanskar ceremony of commitment can be taken whenever a person feels able to understand and take on extra responsibilities and wear the 5Ks.

In the Jewish community, ceremonies take place in the early teens. A boy becomes bar mitzvah at 13 and this is usually marked by taking part in a bar mitzvah ceremony at the synagogue just after his thirteenth birthday. Girls also become bat mitzvah, but at the age of 12 or 13.

© Corbis-Fotolia.com

Bar mitzvah

In the Jewish community a boy is thought to be an adult when he reaches 13. Bar mitzvah, which means 'son of the commandment', is a person who has reached this age. Usually there are special ceremonies on a boy's bar mitzvah day. After this day he is expected to be responsible for his own behaviour.

Usually during the bar mitzvah a boy reads the portion of the Torah for that day. His father or both parents say blessings as the boy becomes a man. The boy will often walk around the synagogue with the Torah scrolls. The boy makes a speech and usually there is a big party. In many Orthodox synagogues this is also the day that a boy is given his tefillin to wear for the first time.

Bat mitzvah

In Orthodox Jewish communities, girls become bat mitzvah which means 'daughter of the commandment' at about the age of 12. They too are expected to be responsible for their own behaviour after this age. A girl will make a speech on the day about the portion of Torah that is being read or on another important topic.

In non-Orthodox Judaism, girls become bat mitzvah at either 12 or 13, depending on the community they belong to, but they read their portion of the Torah in the synagogue in the same way as the boys do at the age of 13. They will also make a speech and, as this is such an important day, there is often a party to celebrate this significant event.

What has been your meaningful milestone in life so far? We would love to hear about your day for our magazine. Please write in with your meaningful milestone so we can share it with our readers.

Find out more about bar and bat mitzvah at www.reonline.org.uk/specials/jwol/

RE Today Services

Sarah

© iStock/3bugsmom.com

We spoke to Sarah just after her big day and asked her to tell us a little bit about it.

Why is your bat mitzvah so important?

My bat mitzvah is important because it is a milestone in the Jewish religion and it is a great personal achievement. It is a sign that I am becoming an adult and have to take on some responsibilities for myself. My bat mitzvah was an amazing weekend which I will never forget!

How do you prepare for your bat mitzvah?

For a year I attended lessons where I learnt about Judaism. In addition to this I also wrote my script which I would read on the day of my bat mitzvah.

What do you have to do in synagogue on the day of your bat mitzvah?

On the day of my bat mitzvah I had to give two speeches to the community. The first was a talk about the portion of the Torah which was being read on that day. The second was a talk on a subject of my choice. I chose to speak about Sarah Schenirer, who was an influential role model and helped introduce Jewish learning to girls and women.

How does the experience of becoming bat mitzvah make you feel?

The experience of my bat mitzvah made me feel proud to be Jewish and proud of completing a year of study. It was enjoyed by my family and friends.

Elliot

Elliot shared with us why his bar mitzvah day was so important to him.

Why is your bar mitzvah so important?

It is a very special event for any Jewish child to become bar or bat mitzvah – it represents the progression from childhood to adulthood within the Jewish religion. When you are classed as an adult you are able to participate more within the services and take a more active role.

How do you prepare for your bar mitzvah?

For a year I had lessons with one of the rabbis from my synagogue. The lessons weren't only for me to learn my portion to be read on the day but to understand many aspects of the Jewish religion and my role within it.

What do you have to do in synagogue on the day of your bar mitzvah?

I gave a synopsis of the portion of the Torah that was being read on that morning, in English so everyone could understand what the service was about. Later I read Maftir and Haftorah which were sections read from the Torah in Hebrew.

When you are in synagogue on the day of your bar mitzvah, will you use any special objects?

I read from the Torah and because you cannot touch the Torah with your hands I used a yad which is a metal pointing hand which was used to keep track of the words. I used the lectern to read my synopsis from and stood on the bimah to read my portion. The bimah is a platform where the morning service is taken from.

When you are in synagogue on the day of your bar mitzvah, do you wear any special garments?

I wore a tallit which is a prayer shawl which all men have to wear when reading from the Torah. I also wore a kippah which is a skull cap that all boys and men wear to cover their heads.

How does the experience of becoming bar mitzvah make you feel?

I feel proud of completing my bar mitzvah after a year of hard work. It was one of the hardest things I have ever had to do!

RE Today
Services   Photocopiable by purchasing institutions

Activity 4 — Writing to improve understanding

The previous three activities prepare pupils to show what they understand and apply what they have learnt in a writing task. While these tasks are good RE tasks, they will also support learning in Literacy and English. Below are three suggested writing activities. Choose the writing style that links with the learning you are doing in English as each of these tasks allows pupils to apply what they have learnt about bar/bat mitzvah and show what they understand about the significance of this milestone in the life of a Jewish person. The final writing task may be suitable for less able or younger pupils.

Information leaflet

Ask pupils to write an information leaflet to be given to children who are 11 and about to prepare for their bar or bat mitzvah. In the information leaflet they must include:

- a description of the preparations they will need to make for the synagogue service
- a description of what will happen in the service
- an explanation of the significance of becoming bar/bat mitzvah and of the specific parts of the ceremony and celebrations
- technical language with definitions, referring to their glossary
- simple organisational devices to ensure their leaflet is easy to read and navigate.

A letter to an uncle

Ask pupils to write an imaginary letter from Sarah or Elliot to a non-Jewish uncle who could not attend the celebrations. In the letter they must include:

- a description of what happened in the service
- an explanation of the significance of becoming bar/bat mitzvah and of the specific parts of the ceremony and celebrations
- technical language with definitions, referring to their glossary.

A postcard of congratulation

Ask pupils to write a postcard to Sarah or Elliot congratulating them on becoming bar or bat mitzvah. In the postcard they must include:

- a description of at least one thing that happened during the service
- their understanding of the significance of becoming bar/bat mitzvah and of the specific parts of the ceremony and celebrations
- technical language with definitions, referring to their glossary.

Activity 5 — Creating a tallit

Remind the children that at bar mitzvah boys often receive their first tallit (prayer shawl); this is then often worn for the rest of their life when attending synagogue. In non-Orthodox synagogues girls sometimes also receive a tallit at bat mitzvah.

As a class, spend some time researching the tallit. Find out what the significance is of the design. Information can be found on websites that sell tallit and on the Jewish Way of Life site:

See: www.reonline.org.uk/specials/jwol/

Research

- the tzitzit (tassles) on each corner of the tallit
- how the prayer shawl design reminds Jewish people of the 613 mitzvot (commandments) that they must follow
- what colours are important
- what material the tallit can be made from.

Design

Arrange pupils in groups with an enlarged version of the tallit template on p.25. Ask them to create an annotated design for a tallit. The annotations should show the significance for Jewish people of their designs. They will need to consider:

- a prayer or blessing to write at the top of the tallit
- how to show the tzitzit reminding Jewish people of the 613 commandments
- the decoration and colour of the garment e.g. tree of life, yad, torah scrolls
- the material that the garment is to be made from.

Create

In groups, create the tallit either on paper or on cloth. Remember if it is being made on cloth it can be either wool or linen or cotton but not a combination of materials as that is prohibited in the Torah.

Once the tallit are completed, display them with an explanation of the significance of their design.

The tallit template is available for NATRE members and RE Today subscribers to download from the RE Today website:

www.retoday.org.uk.

RE Today Services

Creating a tallit

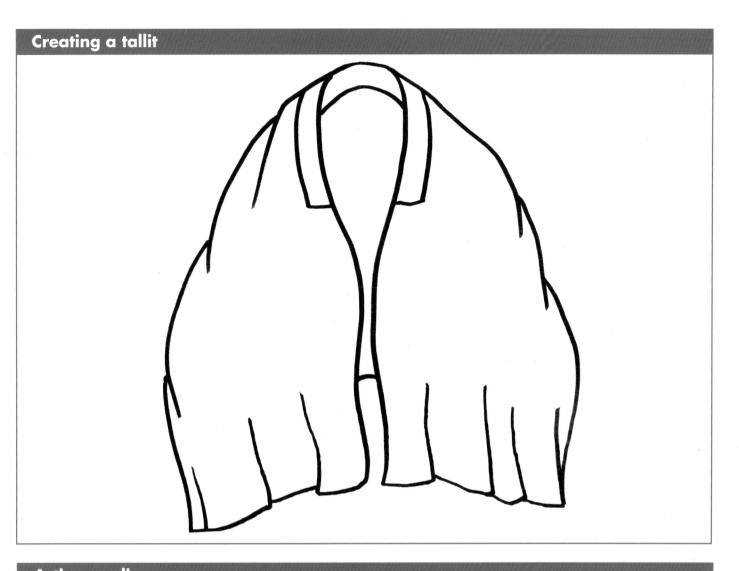

Active reading

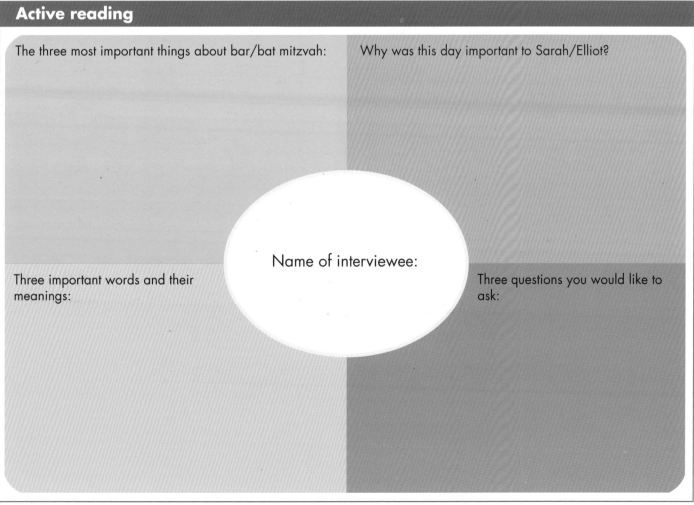

The three most important things about bar/bat mitzvah:

Why was this day important to Sarah/Elliot?

Name of interviewee:

Three important words and their meanings:

Three questions you would like to ask:

Developing debate: hot issues in RE!

Background knowledge for teachers

RE offers an excellent opportunity for pupils to develop their ability to grasp and articulate different viewpoints. As a subject, it deals with contentious issues; it also seeks to promote pupils' attitudes of respect and empathy. These are significant reasons why use of debate is well suited to the RE classroom, where there is always plenty of room for disagreement.

It is important to remember that RE is not about simply letting pupils express their opinions on different matters. Pupils need to be able to show their understanding of religious beliefs and practices, and, when examining questions, be able to back up statements (including their own views) with evidence and argument, in the light of their learning.

This unit offers some strategies for promoting debate, starting with a silent debate strategy for all, through to a full-blown, formal public debate. It uses some real-life contentious scenarios to prompt debate, develop pupils' knowledge and skills in RE.

Links to Literacy and English

The English curriculum (p.32) says, **'mastery of language should be extended through public speaking, performance and debate'.**

RE is an excellent place for honing this mastery of language, where presentation of ideas, questioning, persuasion, analysis and drawing conclusions are all valuable when dealing with matters of disagreement.

Web support

NATRE members and subscribers can also download the following from the RE Today website:

- a copy of the blank snowflake template on p.27
- a copy of a Christianity snowflake to support Activity 2 'Snowflake debate' on p.27.

Assessment for Learning

This section shows some of the outcomes achievable by pupils of different abilities in the 9–11 age range.

Level	Description of achievement: I can ...
3 Almost all pupils in this age group	• make links between religious beliefs, e.g. in ahimsa or the incarnation of Jesus, and behaviour, e.g. Hindu vegetarianism or Christian celebrations of Christmas • *compare my own responses with those of others, e.g. Hindus on being vegetarian, or Christians on 'the real meaning of Christmas'.*
4 Many pupils in this age group	• describe three ways in which belief in God might be demonstrated, e.g. Muslim devotion at mosque, or Christian worship of Jesus at Easter • *refer to the teaching of two religions about God in giving my own response to religious beliefs about God.*
5 The most able pupils in this age group	• explain what it means for a religious believer to believe in e.g. prayer, or life after death, and the impact of this • *explain what may influence and atheist, an agnostic, a Hindu and/or a Christian in the views they hold about God, and what has influenced me.*

This unit helps pupils in Scotland to achieve RME 1-01c and RME 2-02b, RME 2-05b and RME 2-09b.

Essential knowledge for pupils

Pupils should know:

- that there is diversity within and between faith traditions on matters of belief and practice
- that reasonable discussion, using evidence and example, is important in RE, so that people can disagree respectfully
- that people who are part of religious communities do not always believe on the basis of argument – often it is because of upbringing and experience. As faith can guide the whole of a person's life, it is important to take care when exploring and commenting on beliefs and practices.

The following suggestions all offer strategies for promoting debate in RE. They are applicable to almost any situation where there is disagreement within and between people of religious belief, as well as with those who do not follow any particular faith tradition. The six scenarios offered on p.31 give some starting points for debates. As you would expect, they need to accompany some subject knowledge if they are to be anything other than expressions of opinion. Indications of relevant subject knowledge are provided. These activities are designed to be used in different units, you would not use all of them in one unit of work.

 **Silent debate**

 **Snowflake debate**

One way to ensure that you include the introverts as well as the extroverts in your class is to have a 'silent debate'. You need stimulus material to spark off the debate. This might be verses from a relevant poem or short quotations on a topic, for example the Steve Turner poem on p.30 if you are exploring beliefs about life after death, or the quotations on p.30 if you are looking at a philosophical question about the existence of God.

- Put a section of your stimulus material on separate pieces of A3 (or larger) paper on desks or on the walls around the room, or on the back of a roll of wallpaper stretched out across the classroom floor.

- Ask pupils to move silently around the room, writing in black ink their first responses to a phrase or question in the extracts, or to the extract as a whole. They can also comment on other people's comments. Remind pupils that all of this is to be done in silence.

- Give out some coloured pens to different pupils and ask them to add to the comments: blue pens (write questions); red pens (only allowed to challenge comments already made); green pens (qualify and extend comments). This is still a silent debate.

- Call an end to the silence! Ask groups of pupils to take one 'conversation' (one of the large sheets of paper, or a slice of wallpaper, with the annotated texts). Ask them to read the comments and summarise the main responses, so that they can report back briefly to the rest of the class. Put together the poem or sort the quotations into for/against – which statements might represent a religious, agnostic or atheistic view? How do you know?

- As individuals or pairs, pupils produce written responses to the following:

  - Choose two religious figures you have studied and one atheist person you know about. Summarise in 20–30 words each what they might say in response to the poem or the quotations.

  - Write a letter to the poet or one of the writers. Express your own responses to the poem and the poet's beliefs, or the view represented – both critical and creative responses.

A strategy for getting pupils finding reasons for disagreement. Put six or eight statements around a piece of paper, drawing a line into the centre. Pupils mark an X on the line according to how far they agree or disagree with the statement – the closer to the statement, the more they agree. They then join the Xs together with a line, each pupil creating their own unique 'snowflake' outline.

Pupils look at each other's snowflakes and find where they disagree. They then ask each other for good reasons why they think the way they do – they can make a note of their ideas on the paper.

A blank template is shown below. Members and subscribers can download a blank template and an example snowflake on Christianity.

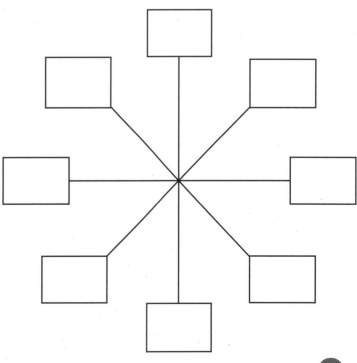

Activity 3 — Human bar chart

This strategy provides another way of allowing pupils to express responses anonymously, and reflect on why pupils have responded differently.

Devise an opinions statement sheet made up of controversial statements on the issue in question. For instance if you are studying religious viewpoints on forgiveness you might use:

- If you turn the other cheek people will think they can be horrid to you.
- Forgiveness is soft – it lets people get away with what they've done wrong.
- Forgiving someone sorts out the problem and lets you get on with things.
- Happy are those who forgive.

Provide a copy for each pupil. Include numbers 1–6 underneath each statement (1 = strongly agree and 6 = strongly disagree) so that pupils can circle a number.

Before the lesson begins, write the numbers 1–6 on A4 sheets and place them in a straight line on the floor or the wall of the classroom or corridor.

Give pupils the opinions statement sheet and ask them to complete it privately, and anonymously, and in pencil. Pupils circle the number which most closely reflects their opinion for each statement. Encourage pupils to express their honest opinions by reassuring them that their responses will be completely anonymous.

Each sheet is then folded in half, and half again, and exchanged five times.

As the teacher reads out the statements, pupils line up in front of the number represented on the sheet they have been given, creating a human barchart.

Pupils, working in groups, e.g. all those with 1 circled on their sheets, work out arguments to support the point of view they are representing. A good debate can arise between those who are 'strongly agreeing' and those who are 'strongly disagreeing'. Can they persuade others in the class to join them or will there be some defectors to the other side?

Activity 4 — Agenda setting

Devise an agenda of questions for small group discussions. The questions could be devised by the teacher or worked out as a class. Provide either a newspaper article or write your own case study exploring a set of issues, such as those set out on p.31. Ask each group to look at the article or case study, considering what it is like for the real people in the situation. The following questions are a suggested selection:

- What is the problem?
- Who is affected?
- Where does it happen?
- How could it be tackled?
- What is the best way forward?
- Who will take action?

A follow-up activity could include working individually or in pairs to write either a balanced argument outlining the different options, or a persuasive text, arguing why one option is better than another. Whole class discussion could focus on: Have you ever experienced a similar conflict in your own life? Who has to take action to solve the conflict?

Activity 5 — Points of view

To build up pupils' capacity to handle formal debating, give them the practice in articulating points of view. Taking an issue where there is disagreement, whether ethical or philosophical, such as the examples on p.31, give pupils a role to take in a discussion. This allows pupils to develop their understanding and empathy for different points of view.

In small groups, number pupils 1–4 or 1–5. All the 1s get together, all the 2s and so on. Give the 1s one point of view, with the information required. Each group prepares their viewpoint together, then make up mixed groups of 1–5s. These mixed groups then have a chance to respond to the chosen issue from the different points of view. Each group can come to a conclusion, and then report back about what their group thinks should be done. Reasons for any differences can be drawn out.

RE Today Services

Activity 6 Ping-Pong and Speed Ping-Pong

Initially, this activity should be done by individuals or pairs of pupils. Give them a starting statement (Ping) and get them to add an opposing point of view (Pong), with a reason for that view. They need to respond to the second statement with an opposing statement (Ping2) and reason, then another response and reason (Pong2). See how far they can get.

A more sophisticated version can include this formula: 'I can see why Ping1 says that because ... but a different point of view (Pong1) would say ... because ...'.

Speed Ping Pong requires a ping-pong ball and some quick reflexes. Pupils stand in a circle, the teacher sets off the controversial statement, throws the ping-pong ball to a pupil who has to say why someone might agree or disagree. They then have to throw it to someone else who has to give an opposing viewpoint, and so on.

Activity 7 Formal debate

All of the earlier strategies help to develop pupils' ability to express and defend a viewpoint. Use several of these strategies as preparation for a formal debate. Formal debate is a way in which pupils can develop their skills in persuading others of their viewpoint. Provide pupils with a carefully worded motion for a debate, or help them develop one of their own. For example:

- This house believes that love of money is a root of all kinds of evil.
- This house believes that prayer is answered.
- This house believes that it would be a better way to show devotion to God if Christians and/or Muslims and/or Jewish people sold their places of worship and used the money to serve those in need.

Two pupils, with supporters, prepare a speech to argue for the motion, and two pupils with supporters prepare a speech against the motion. The speech should last no more than five minutes. Provide pupils with adequate time and resources to prepare their speeches.

Other pupils, also working in small groups, prepare short speeches to be made 'from the floor' to lend support to one side. These speeches should last no more than two minutes. Again, time and resources will need to be provided.

Hold the debate. The four main speakers address the floor first, followed by speeches and questions 'from the floor'.

At the end of the debate a vote is taken and the motion is either 'carried' or 'defeated'.

Pupils, individually or in small groups, prepare a response to the outcome of the debate, reflecting their own considered opinion on the motion. They include a suggestion of how a particular religious group might respond to the motion.

Below are sample resources to start silent debate. These can be used if you are studying beliefs about life after death or a philosophical question about the existence of God. If you are studying another topic, pictures, poems and quotations can all provide suitable material for silent debate.

Heaven

What happens in heaven?
Will I sit on a cloud?
Is walking or talking
Or jumping allowed?

Will I be on my own
Or with some of my friends?
Does it go on for ever
Or eventually end?

What happens in heaven?
Will I play a harp's strings?
I can't play piano
I can't even sing.

Who chooses the music
That angels inspire?
Who does the auditions
For the heavenly choir?

What happens in heaven?
Are the streets paved with gold?
Is it crowded with people
Who're incredibly old?

Will I know who I am?
Will I know what I'm called?
If I pinch myself hard
Will I feel it at all?

What happens in heaven?
Do I go through a gate?
What if I get myself lost
Or turn up too late?

Is my name on a list?
Is the gatekeeper nice?
Can you sneak in for nothing
Or is there a price?

Extract from *Poems* by Steve Turner

Starter stimulus statements for silent debate

I think that the universe is so amazing, it could not have happened by accident! There must be a designer – God!

The Bible tells us about Jesus as the son of God. I think that his life and teachings have been so inspiring to so many millions, it cannot just be fiction.

The world is full of pain and suffering. If there is a god, I do not think that god is a good god.

I think that this is not our only life. After we die we are born again, reincarnated as another human being, or perhaps an animal, depending on how we live this life.

I think there is something special about human beings. We are more than animals, more than machines. I think we have a 'soul'. Perhaps this is what connects us with God.

Human beings are extraordinary. We can create amazing, beautiful art and music; we can invent astonishing technology and heal people through medicine, but we also do such terrible things too.

Faith-based aid organisations are especially committed to serving those in need, often in difficult and dangerous situations such as the Ebola crisis from 2014.

We are all human beings. We all bear responsibility for others. By failing to give to charity, we are indirectly responsible for the suffering of others.

RE Today Services

The following are examples of case studies that are suitable to use for 'Agenda setting', 'Points of view' or 'Formal debate'.

Should Hindus have a day off work or school at Diwali time?

In some areas of the country, schools arrange a closure day for the festival of Diwali. Headteachers have asked that they are allowed to decide which days to mark.

Many schools allow Hindu and Sikh children and staff to have a religious absence day for Diwali.

Christians have both Easter and Christmas as holiday if they work in jobs where they don't have to work shifts.

Can a mosque make a public call to prayer on a Friday?

In a large British city, plans for the call to prayer to be broadcast have caused fierce opposition from local residents.

The mosque elders would like to broadcast a two-minute call to prayer three times a day. Local residents have said their main objection is about a speaker being used; they don't object to the imam calling out the call to prayer. Mosque elders have said if they cannot broadcast the call three times a day they would at least like to be able to broadcast for Friday's Jummah prayer.

Some have said that the call to prayer is like church bells but others have said the call to prayer is different because it states Muslim beliefs.

In a world of inequality and injustice, how should we live?

It is the case that the annual incomes of the world's 100 richest people could end global poverty four times over. In the UK, most of us are in the top 5 per cent of wealthy people in the world. Religions all teach about loving our neighbour and treating others as we would like to be treated. What should we do?

Should Christian Easter mean a holiday for everyone?

As more time is spent thinking about the optimal length of school terms to help children's learning, has the time come to stop giving everybody Easter as a holiday?

Committed Christians could request a religious absence day for Maundy Thursday and we could even consider moving the Good Friday or Easter Monday bank holiday to give an extra break in October.

Should Christmas only be for Christmas?

The real meaning of Christmas is less and less obvious in the way it is celebrated in the UK in the twenty-first century. It's mainly about wanting lots of stuff and eating too much. Very few people are really concerned to celebrate the birth of Jesus Christ as God in the flesh. So, they should keep their hands off it! Christmas for the Christians!

Or does the opportunity for being together as families, giving gifts and sharing mean that it is celebrating the spirit of Christian Christmas by those who are not part of the Christian community? Christmas for all!

Should religious believers be vegetarian?

Some religions teach that human beings should not harm any living creatures (e.g. many Hindus believe in this) and so are vegetarian. The Jewish and Christian scriptures permit the eating of meat, but some argue that caring for God's creation should not include eating or mistreating animals.

There are arguments to say that the raising of cattle for human consumption is one of the biggest causes of greenhouse gases, and in some parts of the world is leading to massive deforestation.

Links to literacy strategies and activities in other curriculum publications

Please note we have chosen only one or two links from the 'Opening up' series of books and the first four books of the 'RE Ideas' series. Most books have many other Literacy strategies listed within them.

Title	Strategy or link to Literacy	Brief description of content
Opening up Values	Understanding the roots of technical vocabulary Interpreting poetry and prayer Writing poetry and prayer	• Key vocabulary from Islam used to understand the Muslim value of peace (5–7) • The Prayer of St Francis of Assisi and 1 Corinthians 13 (7–11)
Opening up Islam	Encouraging pupils to ask and answer questions about texts studied Using similes	• Creative storytelling using two stories from Islam (4–6) • Qur'an similes to consider how a Muslim might describe the Qur'an (7–9)
Opening up Belonging	Examples of recount and role-play strategies Use of metaphor	• Stories of belonging in four religions; a recount of Shabbat and other opportunities to use role play (4–6) • The 'I am' saying about Jesus from the Gospel of John (7–9)
Opening up Hinduism	Drama using shadow puppets	• Exploring the meaning of the Diwali story using shadow puppets and a role-on-wall style activity (6–9)
Opening up Easter	Hotseating, poetry writing and asking questions about a text Interpreting and writing poetry	• The story of Grubby Grub (death and resurrection), hotseating Mary, and writing frames to support poetry writing (7–8) • Poetry on Easter using personification – poetry is used to interpret the Christian understanding of Easter (9–11)
Opening up Respect	Role play including Conscience Alley Using a writing frame to provide reasoned justification for their views	• Solving dilemmas about treating people respectfully using a Querk (4–6) • Structured writing frame to support pupils in expressing their own ideas and the ideas of religious people on living in a world of difference (8–11)
Opening up Judaism	Role play: Conscience Alley Asking questions about a text and suggesting meaning	• Rosh Hashanah and Yom Kippur; interview with a child; 'Conscience Alley' based on Jonah and the Big Fish (7–9) • Interpreting Jewish stories about creation

RE Today Services